DEATH UNCOVERED

RITUALS AND TRADITIONS

Meghan Gottschall

full tilt PRESS

Full Tilt Press
42964 Osgood Road
Fremont, CA 94539
readfulltilt.com

Full Tilt Press publications may be purchased for educational, business, or sales promotional use.

Editorial Credits
Design and layout by Sara Radka
Edited by Nikki Ramsay and Renae Gilles
Copyedited by Emily Cahill and Kristin Russo

Image Credits
Flickr: David Berry, 40, larry&flo, 15; Getty Images: benoitb, 41, Erika Goldring, 32, EyeEm, 23, Fox Photos, 26, HelenL100, cover, Hulton Archive, 18, 20, iStockphoto, 22, 28, Joe Raedle, 35, PhotoStock-Israel, 21, Sean Gardner, 30; Pixabay: Niedec, background (parchment), rawpixel, background (concrete); Shutterstock: Anabela88, 13, Andrey_Kuzmin, 8 (shield), 43 (top), Barandash Karandashich, 3, Everett - Art, 16 (top), Federico Rostagno, 14, Filip Bjorkman, 25, Fresnel, 29, Jim Grant, 10, kimberrywood, 42, Merydolla, 12, Nejron Photo, 9, Pavel Savchuk, 33, Roop_Dey, 5, shimonfoto, 8 (sword), Syda Productions, 24, Vera Petruk, 1, 34, Zdenka Mlynarikova, 6; Wikimedia: George Eastman House, 39, Henrietta Elizabeth Marshall, 8 (top right), Joseph-Siffred Duplessis, 16 (bottom), Rama, 43 (bottom), Unknown, 36, 38

ISBN: 978-1-62920-811-4 (library binding)
ISBN: 978-1-62920-819-0 (ePUB eBook)

CONTENTS

RITUALS AND TRADITIONS

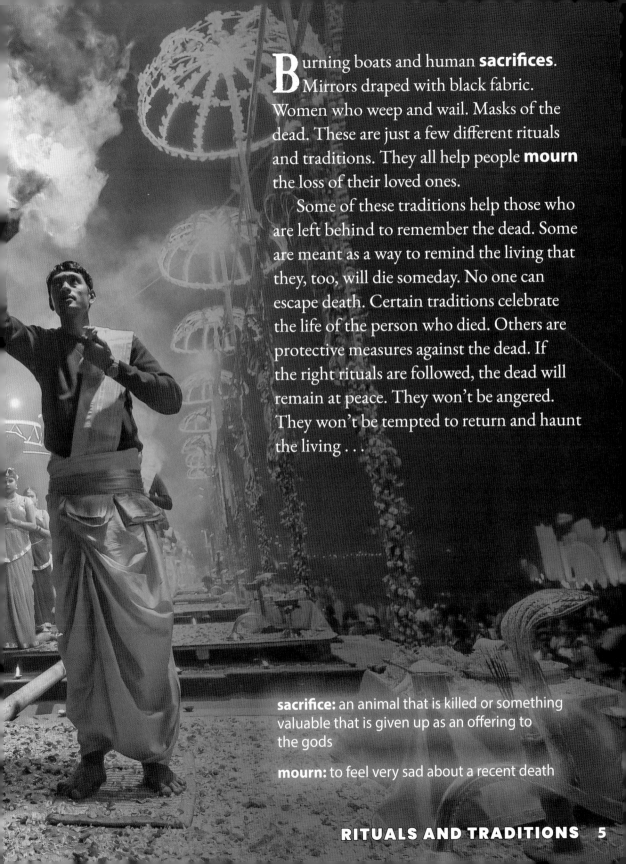

Burning boats and human **sacrifices**. Mirrors draped with black fabric. Women who weep and wail. Masks of the dead. These are just a few different rituals and traditions. They all help people **mourn** the loss of their loved ones.

Some of these traditions help those who are left behind to remember the dead. Some are meant as a way to remind the living that they, too, will die someday. No one can escape death. Certain traditions celebrate the life of the person who died. Others are protective measures against the dead. If the right rituals are followed, the dead will remain at peace. They won't be angered. They won't be tempted to return and haunt the living . . .

sacrifice: an animal that is killed or something valuable that is given up as an offering to the gods

mourn: to feel very sad about a recent death

VIKING FUNERALS

The king of the Vikings' gods, Odin, made a law that all dead people should be burned. Odin said the ashes should then be cast into the sea or buried.

It was year 900. An important Viking leader had died. His followers added sticks and logs to a pile. More wood was needed. The fire would have to burn bright and hot for several hours.

The funeral **pyre** was growing very tall. Later the wood would be set on fire. The leader's body would be burned to ashes. The Vikings believed that the smoke from the fire would help the man reach the **afterlife**.

After the Viking's body was burned on the pyre, his ashes were placed in a longboat. The boat had helped him through life. The Vikings believed it would also help guide him through death.

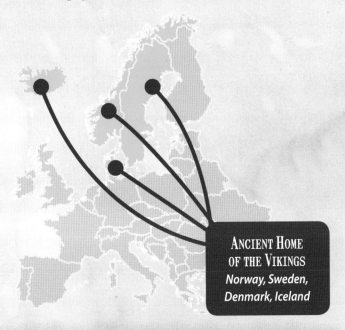

ANCIENT HOME
OF THE VIKINGS
Norway, Sweden, Denmark, Iceland

pyre: a pile of materials that is set on fire, usually to burn a dead body

afterlife: a life which some people believe exists after death

DEATH OF A WARRIOR

In the boat, the Viking leader's belongings had been arranged. They were placed around the **urn** holding his ashes. His sword, shield, and other weapons lay close by. The tools were ready to help him in the afterlife. The ship was decorated with furs and ornaments, such as jewelry and coins. Animals were sacrificed in honor of the great warrior and placed on the ship.

A Viking warrior's weapons were broken before being buried. This helped to cut ties with the land of the living. It also prevented grave robbers from stealing the weapons.

Many Viking funerals required a human sacrifice, if the person who had died was important enough. A **thrall** was killed. They were burned on the funeral pyre with the Viking. Afterwards, the slave might have been buried on the ship. The body might have been placed in a simple grave instead. The thrall was usually a woman. The Vikings believed that she would continue to serve the warrior in the afterlife. Many of these thralls chose their own fates. They volunteered to follow their masters to death—and beyond.

A longship represented a Viking's wealth, power, and even personality, both in life and in death.

urn: a vase-like container used to hold a dead person's ashes

thrall: a slave during the Viking Age (800–1066)

The Vikings believed that the higher the smoke and flames from the funeral, the easier it would be to reach the afterlife.

GRAVE GOODS

For a few of the highest-ranking warriors, a funeral ship was put out to sea. It was then set on fire. Historians believe this type of burial was rare. Ships were too valuable. For most chiefs, ashes and possessions were placed in a simple longboat and then buried.

Choosing the right grave goods was very important to the Vikings. These goods were items that would be useful in the afterlife. Or the items had been important during the person's life. If the right grave goods were not chosen, the dead person might return. They returned as a zombie-like *draugr*, seeking revenge.

Burial Mounds

After a typical Viking funeral, the ashes of the dead were scattered at sea or buried. For a burial, the Vikings placed a mound of dirt over the ashes. The mound is called a *tumulus*. Sometimes they would form the small hill into the shape of a boat. Boats symbolized a safe trip to the afterlife. The Vikings visited the mounds to **pay respects** to the dead. It was a way to honor their memory. Vikings also returned to these sites to pray to their ancestors.

Draugr were also called *aptrganga*, which means "again-walker." They possessed superhuman strength and smelled of rotting flesh. They guarded their graves from anyone who might try to steal from them. Legends said that they were either blue or icy white in color. Fortunately the draugr were not immortal. Their **decaying** bodies did not last forever. Soon they would leave the living in peace.

pay respects: to visit someone in a polite way; to honor a person who has died, usually by attending their funeral

decay: to rot away slowly

DEATH MASKS

King Tut's death mask is made out of gold and precious jewels. It weighs 22 pounds (10 kilograms).

Finally the day had arrived. It was February 16, 1923. Howard Carter and his team of **archaeologists** were in Egypt, in the Valley of the Kings. Three months before, they had discovered the tomb of King Tutankhamen. Slowly and carefully, they had **excavated** the site. At last, they would be able to remove the lid of the coffin, called a sarcophagus. This was where King Tut had been laid to rest. They would finally get to see what lay inside.

A shimmer of gold caught their attention first. It was the death mask of King Tutankhamen. Carter was the first person to see it in more than 3,000 years. The mask showed the facial features of the king. It had also been carved with symbols representing Osiris. Osiris is the ancient Egyptian god of the afterlife.

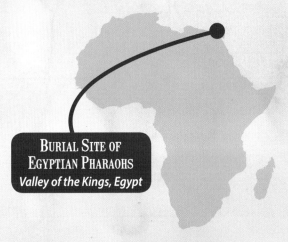

BURIAL SITE OF EGYPTIAN PHARAOHS
Valley of the Kings, Egypt

archaeologist: a scientist who studies the bones, tools, and buildings of ancient people

excavate: to uncover by digging out of the earth

REMEMBERING THE DEAD

The mask had been placed over the king's **mummified** body. Death masks were an important part of death rituals in ancient Egypt and other parts of Africa. The masks were believed to strengthen the spirit. They helped the spirit arrive in the underworld unharmed. Many Egyptians had death masks made. Few were as ornate as King Tut's.

Ancient Egyptians weren't the only people to use death masks. In Europe between the years 500 and 1300, death masks were made for members of royal families. The mask was placed over the covered body during a funeral.

Starting in the 1300s, a doctor or sculptor would make the mask.

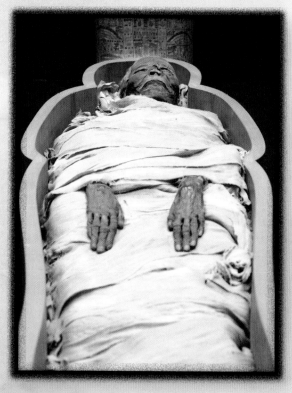

For the ancient Egyptians, the process of making a mummy took about 70 days.

They placed plaster or wax onto the dead person. The mask would be an exact copy of their face. Sometimes a sculptor would create a sculpture of the dead person. They would use their mask as a model. Death masks and sculptures were a way to honor the dead by keeping their memory alive.

mummified: preserved after death, especially by ancient Egyptians by being wrapped in cloth

Italian poet Dante Alighieri's *Divine Comedy* tells the story of his visit to the realms of the dead. Dante died in 1321. Today his death mask is on display in Florence, Italy.

FAMOUS DEATH MASKS

Starting in the 1700s, death masks became more popular. But they were still usually used for famous people. Death masks were made for Napoleon and Beethoven. So did Benjamin Franklin. Mary Queen of Scots also had a mask. She ruled Scotland from 1542 to 1567. People wanted to remember what these famous people had looked like in life. This was important in a time before photography.

Benjamin Franklin died in 1790.

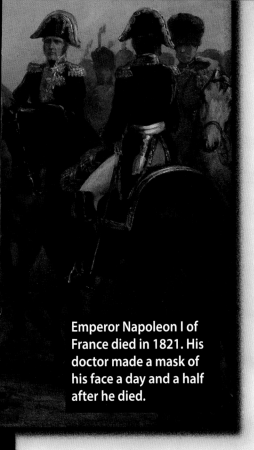

Emperor Napoleon I of France died in 1821. His doctor made a mask of his face a day and a half after he died.

Shakespeare's Death Mask?

In 1849, a death mask was found in Germany. Many people thought it looked like William Shakespeare, a famous playwright. The mask was dated 1616. That is the same year Shakespeare died. Today many experts believe the mask is a fake. At that time, it was rare for someone who wasn't a member of the royal family to have a death mask made. To this day, no one is sure what Shakespeare looked like.

Another famous death mask was made of bank robber John Dillinger. In life, Dillinger disguised his identity. He had had multiple **plastic surgeries**. In 1934, the FBI finally caught up with him. Some people thought that Dillinger had made a great escape. They said someone else had been killed in his place. Dillinger's death mask was examined by many people after his death. They were trying to determine if it was really him. Even his own father said he didn't recognize him. The FBI finally ran tests. The tests determined it was Dillinger who had died.

Death masks have sometimes been used as evidence in criminal cases. Sometimes masks were made of people whose identities were unknown when they died. Police hoped that this would be a way to identify the body later.

plastic surgery: a type of surgery that changes or restores the body, often after injury

COVERED MIRRORS

THE NATION MOURNS.

President Abraham Lincoln was killed in 1865. Afterwards, many of the mirrors in the White House were covered in black fabric.

After the old woman died, her family covered all of the mirrors in her home with black **shrouds**. No one could look into the mirrors. But more importantly, nothing could look back out of the mirrors either.

Many different cultures have covered mirrors or turned them around to face the wall after someone has died. This was a common practice in Europe and the United States. It was popular in the 18th and 19th centuries. It was most popular in the early 18th and 19th centuries. But it is also something that is still practiced today. It is an important part of Jewish mourning rituals. The tradition still lives on in Poland, as well.

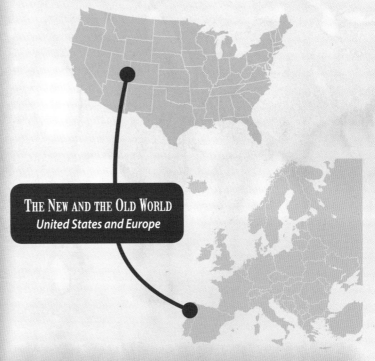

THE NEW AND THE OLD WORLD
United States and Europe

shroud: a piece of heavy cloth or other material that covers and hides something

DANGEROUS MIRRORS

So why might covering mirrors be important after a death? Some believed that the spirit of the person who died would see itself in a mirror. Then it might become trapped. The spirit could be turned into a **vengeful** ghost. Or it might simply be confused. It would be unable to move on to the afterlife. If the dead person saw themselves in a mirror and realized they were dead, they would be shocked. They would be unable to rest peacefully.

Until the late 19th century in the United States, most funerals were held at the home of the person who died.

vengeful: wanting to harm a person who has harmed you

Modern mirrors were invented in the 1830s. Since then, some people have believed they serve as portals to the spirit world.

Another belief was that after a death, the first person to see themselves in a mirror would be the next to die. Some believed the soul stayed inside the house for three days after death. Mirrors needed to be covered immediately. These are frightening possibilities. No one wanted to take the chance of not covering a house's mirrors.

Gravestones have been used to mark the resting place of the dead since 3,000 BC.

NO DISTRACTIONS

There is also another, more practical reason why mirrors might be covered. Friends and family would be able to mourn without worrying about how they looked. They would be free to cry or become emotional. Mourners would not be distracted by their own appearance. This was also a way to keep people from acting vain. It stopped them from only thinking about themselves. Instead, they thought of the person who had died.

Time of Death

There are many traditions that occur after someone dies at home. One is to stop the clocks at the hour of death. This was very common in the 19th century. It was done in Europe and the United States. People believed it would prevent more bad luck for the family. Or it would help the dead person pass on to the afterlife. Others viewed it as an easy way to remember the exact time of death.

Today, some people still cover mirrors after a death. The tradition is practiced today by people of the Jewish faith. Mirrors are covered for seven days during Shiva. This is the official period of mourning for the dead. The tradition encourages people to reflect. They think about the life of the dead person instead of themselves. Mourners should also reflect on the nature of death. They think about their relationship with God during the time of grief. Mirrors are seen as a distraction to this way of thinking.

PROFESSIONAL
MOURNERS

Crying after the death of a loved one can be an important part of grieving. Scientists believe crying helps with physical and emotional pain.

The woman was dressed all in black. All of a sudden, her body bent as if she were in pain. Her mouth opened. She started to wail. She grabbed at her clothing. The clothes started to rip. She pulled on her hair and scratched her face. She pounded the ground with her fists. She wept loudly. Tears rolled down her face, but she didn't wipe them away. She left them streaming down her face. Soon other women near her were doing the same thing. The women joined a funeral **procession**. They followed a casket down the street.

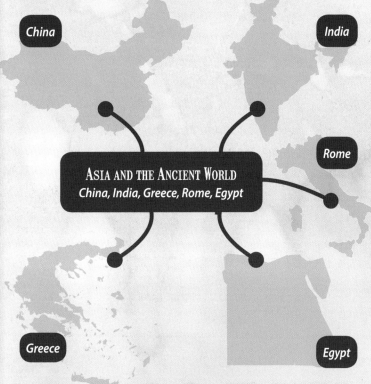

China

India

Rome

ASIA AND THE ANCIENT WORLD
China, India, Greece, Rome, Egypt

Greece

Egypt

procession: a group of people or vehicles that follow in a line slowly

More than 2 million people attended the funeral for Indian statesman Mahatma Gandhi in 1948. The procession stretched for 5 miles (8 km).

A LONG TRADITION

An outsider might have thought these women had lost someone dear to them. However, the women did not even know who had died. They had been hired as professional mourners. These were people who were paid to weep and wail during funerals.

Professional mourners have been used for many reasons. People hired them to increase funeral sizes. This showed off their wealth and power. The ancient Romans wanted loud funeral processions. Noise meant an important person had died.

Sometimes professional mourners were hired so that no one would be afraid to be the first to cry and express their emotions. The weeping and grief were meant to encourage others to join in.

Professional mourners can be found throughout history. In China, the tradition dates back to the 3rd century or earlier. Ancient Greeks and Romans used hired mourners. Egyptians did too. Mourners were seen at funeral **rites** and processions. In Europe, the tradition was popular until the 19th century.

rite: a religious act or ceremony

MOURNERS TODAY

In India, the tradition is still popular. It is found in the northwestern state of Rajasthan. Professional mourners there are often women of a low social class. Women from higher social classes are expected to hide their emotions. Yet to respect the dead, someone must express feelings of loss.

In Europe and the United States, modern professional mourners are often actors. They are hired to increase the crowd at a funeral. Today, though, they try to blend in as real mourners. They often study the part like they would for an acting role.

The tradition of professional mourning in China has been going on for more than 2,000 years. Today some mourners sing and dance. It is almost like a play at the theater.

Tradition of Keening

The tradition of keening was popular in Ireland from the 1500s until the 1950s. Keeners let out death wails at funerals or burial sites. Sometimes keening would include chanting. They chanted praises for the person who had died. Or they cried out about the sadness of those left behind. The wailing could sound like singing. But it was out of tune and unpleasant. Keeners were often paid a small amount of money. Or they were given dinner as payment.

Today, many people wear black to funerals in the United States and Europe. In the 19th century, people would wear black mourning clothes for six months to a year.

NEW ORLEANS JAZZ FUNERALS

Musicians play tambourines and joyful songs during the second part of a jazz funeral.

A brass band marches down the street. Upbeat jazz music fills the air. A crowd follows the band. They dance and sing along to the music. Everyone seems happy. The atmosphere is like a party. Spectators watch from the sidelines and join. But this is no ordinary parade or celebration. This is a New Orleans jazz funeral.

A jazz funeral often starts at the home of the person who died. Sometimes it starts at a funeral home. At first, the band plays sad music. The musicians play **dirges** and religious songs. Family and friends slowly follow the band. They go to the cemetery to bury their loved one.

BIRTHPLACE OF JAZZ
New Orleans, Louisiana

dirge: a sad song that honors the dead

CUTTING LOOSE

At the cemetery, the body is laid to rest. After the burial, everything changes. Burying the body during a New Orleans jazz funeral is called "cutting the body loose." Once that is complete, the crowd can "cut loose" too. The music picks up speed. The band plays happier songs. At first, people's expressions were sad and somber. Now they are upbeat and hopeful. A jazz funeral helps celebrate the life of the person who died.

The music from a jazz funeral attracts strangers and tourists who want to join the celebration.

The band and friends and family of the person who died are known as the "first line." Members of the crowd who join the procession are called the "second line." These are strangers. They want to help celebrate the memory of the person who died. The crowd parades through the streets. Sometimes it goes for hours. People dance in the streets. They play tambourines and drums along with the marching band.

Voodoo priests and priestesses use many tools during their rituals. They may use candles, incense, powders, dolls, or charms called *gris-gris*.

A DIVERSE HISTORY

Many different influences brought about New Orleans jazz funerals. The tradition is rooted in West African rituals. The rituals were brought to the United States by enslaved people. This was in the 18th and 19th centuries. Music played an important role in West African funerals. Music and chanting helped mourners celebrate the life of the deceased. Mourners would dance in an inner circle. Children would form a second, outer circle for dancing.

After slavery ended in the United States, military brass bands became popular. Bands would often play at funerals. Then jazz music became popular in the 1930s. The songs these bands played started to change.

Voodoo Death Ritual

Voodoo is a religion from Haiti and Louisiana. There are many rituals that must be performed after someone dies. Practitioners believe that the soul enters the spirit world immediately after death. But it stays close to the body for the first week. After seven to nine days, a Voodoo priest or priestess performs a ritual. The Nine-Night Ritual frees the soul from the body. The soul rests for a year and a day. Then the Rite of **Reclamation** is performed. This allows the soul to be reborn into the next generation.

Jazz funerals were originally held when a musician died. Other musicians honored them through music. Then the tradition spread to other people. Today, jazz funerals aren't quite as common as they used to be. But they're still held for prominent New Orleans musicians and figures. They are also held for young people who pass away too soon.

reclamation: the act of making something old useful again

In New Orleans, music is a part of life and death.

POST-MORTEM PHOTOGRAPHS

In Victorian England, the average age of death was 35.

Photography was an exciting new medium during the Victorian era in England (1837–1901). Suddenly people had a way to look back at any day they chose. A wedding, a family gathering . . . even a funeral.

The first photographs of the dead were taken of people in coffins. A coffin was usually in the dead person's own home. A photo could then be kept by friends and family. The photo was a way to remember the deceased. Sometimes it would be the only photograph ever taken of the person.

The photos reminded those left behind of the person who had died. They also served as a *memento mori*. In Latin, this means "Remember that you, too, will die."

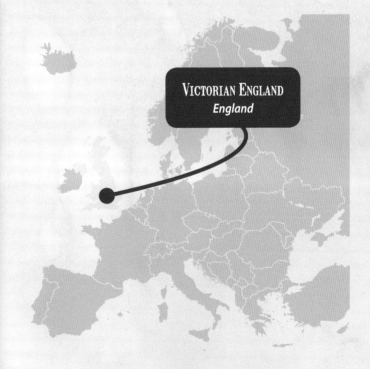

VICTORIAN ENGLAND
England

Devices to hold up the dead were often hidden in chairs or behind curtains.

MEMENTO MORI

Memento mori were usually paintings. Sometimes they were objects, such as jewelry. They were first popular in medieval times. The mementos gained popularity during the Victorian era. They served as a reminder that death is **inevitable**. They allowed people to think about the nature of death. They could come to terms with the idea of dying.

Victorian **post-mortem** photographs became the newest type of *memento mori*. Soon photographers began to get more creative. They took pictures of the dead in new ways. They would prop up the dead person. Then they would photograph the body alongside living family members. Victorian cameras were still very slow. It took a long time to take a picture. Any slight movement would affect the final photograph. This meant that the dead person often appeared the most sharply in focus. They had been entirely still. The living subjects of the photograph were often blurry.

The earliest photographs were taken in the 1820s.

inevitable: going to happen and unable to be avoided

post-mortem: after death

Victorians were fascinated with death. People had picnics in cemeteries. Large funerals were held. Even household animals would wear a black ribbon to show that a family was in mourning.

PHOTO EFFECTS

For post-mortem photographs, the dead were sometimes placed in sitting or standing positions. Photographers used special chairs or stands. These devices were often hidden from view. They would not appear in the final photograph.

Sometimes photographers painted directly onto the photo to achieve different effects. They wanted to make the dead person look alive again. They would paint open eyes onto the eyelids of the dead person in the photo. Or they would add some color to the cheeks. This was an early type of photo editing. It can be difficult to tell if the people in these photos are dead or alive.

Funeral Hair Art

During the Victorian era in England, women started to collect locks of hair from dead loved ones. It was as a way to remember them. They turned the hair into small works of art. Artworks included wreaths. They were kept at home. Sometimes women turned the hair into jewelry that they could wear. Women often worked together to make these pieces. It was a way to mourn together. They could share memories of the person who had died.

Another type of photography of the dead became common during the American Civil War (1861–1865). However, photographers weren't taking portraits of the dead in their homes. Instead, for the first time, they were able to photograph battlefields. These pictures showed the horrors of war. They sent the message that some deaths should be avoided.

Sometimes, stands were used to help even the living hold still for photos.

RITUALS AND TRADITIONS FACTS

Originally NEW ORLEANS musicians didn't like the phrase "jazz funeral." Instead they preferred "funeral with music." They thought it was better for a serious occasion.

In a New Orleans jazz funeral, "WHEN THE SAINTS GO MARCHING IN" is one of the most popular songs that is played.

PROFESSIONAL MOURNERS are called "moirologists."

In recent times, there was a company in the UK called RENT A MOURNER. It allowed families to find professional mourners. The service increased funeral ATTENDANCE.

The VIKINGS believed that burning the dead with the goods they possessed in life allowed them to maintain their social status in death.

In many cultures, dead bodies are carried out of the house FEET-FIRST. It is believed that this prevents the dead person from returning as an ANGRY SPIRIT.

HENRY IV of France died in 1610. But a death mask of his face wasn't made until 180 YEARS later, during the middle of the French Revolution.

Soon after his death, NAPOLEON'S death mask was stolen. When it was returned, people weren't sure if it was the original. The DEATH MASK seemed to have different features than paintings of Napoleon. The mask is currently on display near Napoleon's tomb. Many people still have doubts about it.

QUIZ

1 Who did Vikings pray to at *tumulus* burial mounds?

2 What is King Tut's death mask made of?

3 How have death masks been used in criminal cases?

4 When were mirrors invented?

5 The tradition of keening was practiced in which country?

6 Who were jazz funerals originally held for?

7 What does *memento mori* mean?

8 What are professional mourners called?

ANSWERS
1. Their ancestors
2. Gold and precious jewels
3. As a way to identify bodies later
4. In the 1830s
5. Ireland
6. Musicians who died
7. "Remember that you, too, will die."
8. Moirologists

ACTIVITY

Research a modern ritual or tradition.

Death rituals aren't only something that occurred in the past. Today many cultures perform rituals when someone dies. Some of these traditions have existed for centuries. In this activity, you will research a modern death ritual and write a report.

What you will need:

MATERIALS NEEDED

- Group of two to three friends or classmates
- Library or internet access
- Pencils and paper

STEPS

1 Pick a country or part of the world that interests you.

2 Use the library or the internet to research a death ritual that people perform there today.

3 Take notes on what you find.

4 With your partners, answer the following questions.

- What are the different steps to the ritual?
- Who performs the ritual?
- Are any specific objects needed?
- What is the ritual's connection to history?

5 Use your answers to these questions to write a one-page report.

6 Share your research with your friends and classmates.

GLOSSARY

afterlife: a life which some people believe exists after death

archaeologist: a scientist who studies the bones, tools, and buildings of ancient people

decay: to rot away slowly

dirge: a sad song that honors the dead

excavate: to uncover by digging out of the earth

inevitable: going to happen and unable to be avoided

mourn: to feel very sad about a recent death

mummified: preserved after death, especially by ancient Egyptians by being wrapped in cloth

pay respects: to visit someone in a polite way; to honor a person who has died, usually by attending their funeral

plastic surgery: a type of surgery that changes or restores the body, often after injury

post-mortem: after death

procession: a group of people or vehicles that follow in a line slowly

pyre: a pile of materials that is set on fire, usually to burn a dead body

reclamation: the act of making something old useful again

rite: a religious act or ceremony

sacrifice: an animal that is killed or something valuable that is given up as an offering to the gods

shroud: a piece of heavy cloth or other material that covers and hides something

thrall: a slave during the Viking Age (800–1066)

urn: a vase-like container used to hold a dead person's ashes

vengeful: wanting to harm a person who has harmed you

READ MORE

Ganeri, Anita. *Remembering the Dead around the World.* Cultures and Customs. Chicago: Heinemann Raintree, 2016.

Hollihan, Kerrie Logan. *Mummies Exposed!* Creepy and True. New York: Abrams Books for Young Readers, 2019.

Machajewski, Sarah. *Death Rituals.* Digging Up the Dead. New York: Gareth Stevens Publishing, 2015.

INTERNET SITES

https://www.neworleans.com/things-to-do/music/history-and-traditions/jazz-funeral
Read about New Orleans jazz funerals, and see photographs from processions.

https://norse-mythology.org
Find out more about the gods, stories, and traditions of the Viking Age.

http://oi-archive.uchicago.edu/OI/MUS/ED/mummy.html
Follow the steps of the mummification tradition with an interactive game.

INDEX